COLECCIÓN AGOSTO 2020

Bajo acuerdo con Under Music Flow

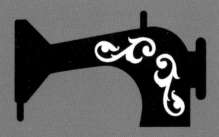

MACPHERSON MERCH STORE

WE ARE YOUR STORE

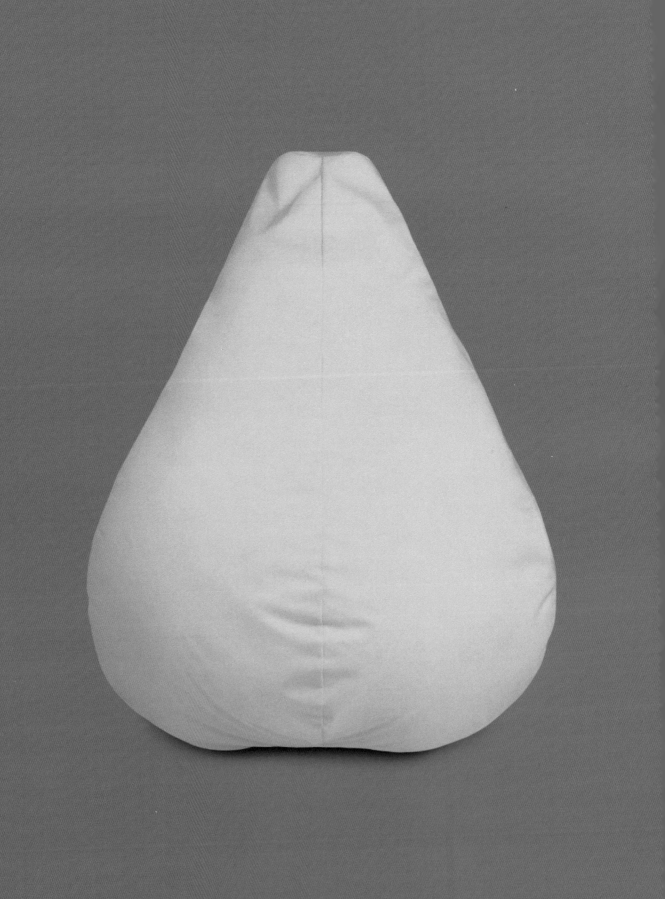

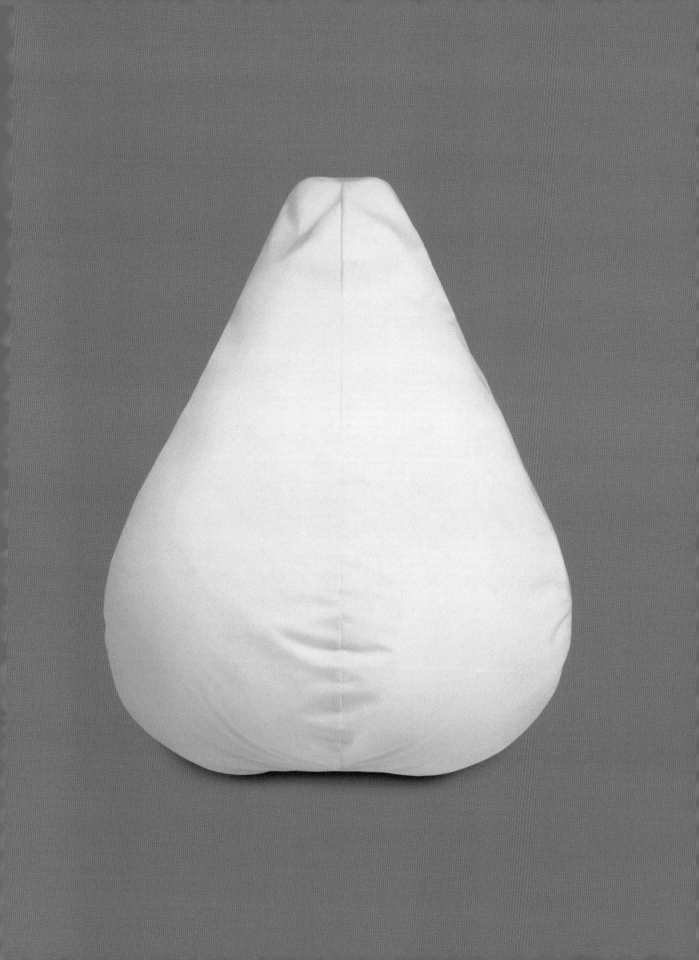

Charmed

MACPHERSON MERCH STORE

WE ARE YOUR STORE

Charmed

MACPHERSON MERCH STORE

WE ARE YOUR STORE

CPSIA information can be obtained at www.ICGtesting.com
Printed in the USA
LVIW012302261020
669912LV00004B/8